America, My Country
American Heroes

George Washington

By Ashleigh Hally

Clarke C. Scott, M.A.
Content Consultant

STATE STANDARDS PUBLISHING®

Your State • Your Standards • Your Grade Level

Dear Educators, Librarians and Parents . . .

Thank you for choosing books from State Standards Publishing! This book supports state Departments of Educations' standards for elementary level social studies and has been measured by the ATOS Readability Formula for Books (Accelerated Reader), the Lexile Framework for Reading, and the Fountas & Pinnell Benchmark Assessment System for Guided Reading. Photographs and/or illustrations, captions, and other design elements have been included to provide supportive visual messaging to enhance text comprehension. Glossary and Word Index sections introduce key new words and help young readers develop skills in locating and combining information. "Think With Bagster" questions provide teachers and parents with tools for additional learning activities and critical thinking development. We wish you all success in using this book to meet your student or child's learning needs.

Jill Ward, President

Publisher

State Standards Publishing, LLC
1788 Quail Hollow
Hamilton, GA 31811
USA
1.866.740.3056
www.statestandardspublishing.com

Library of Congress Control Number: 2011931742

ISBN-13: 978-1-935884-45-3 (hardcover)
ISBN-13: 978-1-935884-54-5 (paperback)

Printed in the United States of America, North Mankato, Minnesota, August 2011, 060611.

1 2 3 4 5 - CG - 15 14 13 12 11

About the Author

Ashleigh Hally has a degree in English literature from the University of Georgia. She has been a library assistant and copywriter and is currently working on a manuscript for the young adult market. She currently teaches reading and writing to elementary students in the Atlanta area. Ashleigh enjoys traveling and spending time with her husband, Patrick, and their three children.

About the Content Consultant

Clarke C. Scott holds degrees from Central Michigan University and has 31 years of experience as a classroom teacher, building principal and system-wide administrator. Clarke currently serves as Director of Middle School Education and Lead Director for History with Pittsylvania County Schools in Virginia. He enjoys hiking, kayaking, caving, and exploring Virginia's and our nation's history. He shares his adventures both above and underground with his wife, Joyce, and three grown children.

Table of Contents

George surveyed the land.

Time Line

1732 Born

1748 Starts surveying

A Life of Adventure

George Washington was born in Virginia. George liked math. He learned to **survey**. He measured the land. He surveyed land in western Virginia. He was only sixteen. He traveled for many weeks. George wrote in his diary. He wrote about his trip. Once he slept under a blanket with lice and fleas!

George went to protect Virginia.

Time Line

1732 Born

1748 Starts surveying

1753 – Goes on mission

George, the Soldier

George became a soldier. He went to the Ohio River. He went on a **mission**. He went to protect Virginia. The mission was dangerous. George fell out of a boat. The river was icy. He almost drowned! But George was not afraid. He was a good leader. Men trusted him. George wrote about the mission. He became famous.

George farmed on his plantation.

Time Line

1732 Born

1748 Starts surveying

1753 – Goes on mission

1758 Goes home

George, the Farmer

George went home. He married Martha Custis. They lived on his **plantation**. It was a big farm. It was called Mount Vernon. George was a good farmer. He grew wheat. He sold the flour. He grew many other crops, too. He rode his horse every day. He liked to hunt with his dogs.

People asked George to lead the army.

Time Line

1732 Born

1748 Starts surveying

1753 – Goes on mission

1758 Goes home

Leading the Army

The king of England ruled America. People in America paid **taxes** to England. They paid money to the king. They paid taxes on many things, like tea and sugar. People did not want England to rule America. They did not want to pay taxes. They were ready to fight. George was brave and strong. They asked him to lead the army.

1775
Leads army

George's men surprised the English soldiers.

Time Line

1732 Born

1748 Starts surveying

1753 – Goes on mission

1758 Goes home

George Wins!

Many soldiers came from England. There were not many soldiers for America. George was clever. He was smart. The English soldiers stood in straight lines. They wore red coats. George's men hid in the woods. They surprised the English soldiers. The war lasted many years. George's army won the war!

1775 Leads army

1783 Wins war

The people chose George to be president.

Time Line

1732 Born

1748 Starts surveying

1753 – Goes on mission

1758 Goes home

Our First President

America was a new nation. The people needed a leader. They **voted**. They chose a leader. They chose George. He was the first **president** of the United States. He led the country. He worked hard to make America strong.

1775 Leads army

1783 Wins war

1789 Becomes president

George helped start Washington, D. C.

Time Line

1732 Born

1748 Starts surveying

1753 – Goes on mission

1758 Goes home

A New Capital

America needed a **capital**. It needed a place for the government to work. George helped start Washington, D. C. Workers built the president's house. Today it is called the White House. The house was not finished in time. George never lived in the White House.

1775 Leads army
1783 Wins war
1789 Becomes president
1790 – Starts Washington, D. C.

George said goodbye. He went home to Mount Vernon.

Time Line

1732 Born

1748 Starts surveying

1753 – Goes on mission

1758 Goes home

George Goes Home

George was president for eight years. People asked him to be president again. George was an honest man. He did not want the president to be like a king. He said eight years was enough. George said goodbye. He went home to Mount Vernon.

1775 Leads army

1783 Wins war

1789 Becomes president

1790 – Starts Washington, D. C.

1797 Goes home

George was the *Father of Our Country*.

Time Line

1732 Born

1748 Starts surveying

1753 – Goes on mission

1758 Goes home

The Father of Our Country

George rode around his farm one December. It was snowing and sleeting. George got very sick. Martha sat next to his bed. George told her, "I die hard, but I am not afraid to go." George was a great leader. He was the *Father of Our Country*.

1775 Leads army
1783 Wins war
1789 Becomes president
1790 – Starts Washington, D. C.
1797 Goes home
1799 Dies

Glossary

capital – The city where a government works.

mission – A special job or task.

plantation – A big farm.

president – A person who leads the country.

survey – To measure land in order to make a map or plan.

taxes – Money paid to support a government.

vote – To choose a leader.

Word Index

Editorial Credits

Designer: Michael Sellner, Corporate Graphics, North Mankato, Minnesota
Consultant/Marketing Design: Alison Hagler, Basset and Becker Advertising, Columbus, Georgia

Image Credits – *All images © copyright contributor below unless otherwise specified.*

Cover – North Wind Picture Archives. **4/5** – North Wind Picture Archives. **6/7** – North Wind Picture Archives. **8/9** – "Life of George Washington, the Farmer" painting by Junius Brutus Stearns/Wikipedia. **10/11** – JVPD/ImageEnvision. **12/13** – North Wind Picture Archives. **14/15** – Alamy. **16/17** – New York Public Library/Stephen A. Schwarzman Building/Print Collection, Miriam & Ira D. Wallach Division of Art, Prints and Photographs. **18/19** – New York Public Library, Mid-Manhattan Library/Picture Collection. **20/21** – North Wind Picture Archives.

Think With Bagster

1. Why do you think George was a good soldier? How was he a strong leader?

2. George kept a diary. Why is it helpful that he wrote about his life? What are some ways people use diaries today?

3. Why do you think the people chose George to be the first president? Would he make a good president today? Why or why not?

4. Why do you think George would not be president longer than eight years?